HOW TO TRAIN YOUR BRAIN TO OVERCOME FEAR AND DOUBT

Stop Overthinking, Build Our Mindset

By

Keaton Beckwith

"A healthy outside starts
from the inside."

- Robert Urich

Table of Contents

INTRODUCTION

In the intricate shade of human existence, fear and doubt frequently crop as redoubtable walls, hindering the pursuit of bournes and stifling the eventuality of growth. The mortal mind, with its complicated complications, possesses an inconceivable capacity for both brilliance and tone-assessed limitations. This book is drafted with the intent of unraveling the intricate vestments of apprehension that weave through the cognitive fabric.

Embarking on this transformative trip requires a deep dive into the nuanced terrain of fear and mistrustfulness, understanding their birth, and decoding the intricate interplay between studies and feelings. The mortal mind, akin to an ever-evolving geography, is susceptible to the influences of both external and internal factors. These companion trials serve as a compass, guiding compendiums through the uncharted home of their minds, offering perceptivity and strategies to navigate the tumultuous swell of fear and mistrustfulness.

The trip commences with a disquisition of the profound impact of mindset on our lives. The contradiction between a fixed and growth mindset sets the stage for understanding how our internal fabrics shape our responses to challenges and lapses. Identification forms the bedrock of conquering any adversary. therefore, the posterior sections unfold as a strategic design for defying and prostrating these internal hurdles.

Challenging limiting beliefs is a vital step in this transformative process. This companion unfolds as a primer for internal addition, furnishing practical exercises and real-life exemplifications to empower compendiums in reshaping their cognitive armature. Embracing failure, frequently synonymous with fear, emerges as a foundation of adaptability. Cultivating a healthy relationship with failure becomes a means to perceive it not as a stumbling block but as a stepping gravestone toward particular growth. awareness, a conception decreasingly honored for its remedial graces, takes center stage. ways of contemplation and awareness are unveiled as potent tools to calm the stormy swell of the mind, fostering clarity and concentration in the face of adversity. Adaptability, bandied then, becomes the sturdy vessel navigating the changeable waters of life, furnishing compendiums with the means to rebound from lapses.

Strategic thing- setting offers a roadmap for compendiums to cut the path from aspiration to consummation. By breaking down larger objects into manageable tasks, compendiums can cultivate a sense of accomplishment, dismembering the fear and mistrustfulness that frequently accompany dispiriting trials. The influential power of our surroundings is unwrapped. The connections we cultivate significantly impact our internal geography. This companion serves as a primer to creating a positive support network, a fort against the rush of negativity. Visualization, a frequently- undervalued fashion, is unveiled as an important instrument for shaping a positive mindset. Mental practices of success come as the precursor to palpable achievements, fostering confidence in the face of mistrustfulness. Cultivating tone- compassion emerges as an attar for the injuries foisted by fear and mistrustfulness, promoting a nurturing inner dialogue that fosters adaptability. Taking action despite fear constitutes the crux. Procrastination and avoidance, the silent abettors of fear, are brazened head-on with practical strategies for breaking indolence and initiating positive change. Learning from success becomes a compass guiding compendium through the terrain of triumphs, unraveling the complications of replicating success. Celebrating progress invites compendiums to admit the incremental palms that pave the way for sustained confidence. The trip culminates then, where sustaining a positive mindset becomes the foundation of long-term internal well-being. Compendiums are equipped with strategies to weave these transformative practices into the fabric of their diurnal lives, fostering perpetual growth and adaptability against the ever-present specters of fear and mistrustfulness.

As we embark on this odyssey of tone- -discovery, let this companion be trusted, a lamp illuminating the path toward a mindset liberated from the impediment of fear and mistrustfulness. Through soul-searching, adaptability, and purposeful action, let us unravel the idle eventuality within, training our smarts to transcend the limitations that have, for too long, hindered the consummation of our most profound aspirations.

Chapter 1

UNDERSTANDING FEAR AND DOUBT

Fear and doubt are powerful emotions that can profoundly impact our lives, shaping our thoughts, actions, and overall well-being. In this chapter, we delve into the intricate dynamics of fear and doubt, aiming to unravel their complexities and provide a foundation for overcoming their pervasive influence.

Fear, often viewed as a natural response to perceived threats, has deep evolutionary roots. It served our ancestors well, alerting them to potential dangers and ensuring survival in hostile environments. However, in today's complex world, fear can manifest in various forms – from rational concerns to irrational anxieties that hinder personal growth.

Doubt, on the other hand, is the inner skeptic questioning our abilities, decisions, and self-worth. It often arises from a lack of confidence, past failures, or external influences. Understanding the roots of doubt is crucial in dismantling its barriers and fostering a mindset of self-assurance.

To grasp the impact of fear and doubt on our mental health, consider the story of Sarah, a professional navigating the competitive world of entrepreneurship. Sarah's fear of failure and doubt in her capabilities became so overwhelming that they paralyzed her ability to make crucial decisions. As we explore Sarah's journey, we gain insights into the real-life consequences of these emotions.

In examining the psychological underpinnings of fear and doubt, it becomes evident that they share common cognitive processes. The intricate dance between our thoughts and emotions plays a pivotal role in perpetuating these negative cycles. Cognitive distortions, such as catastrophizing and overgeneralization, can magnify fears and amplify doubts, creating a self-reinforcing loop that stifles personal development.

Acknowledging the detrimental effects of fear and doubt is the first step towards building resilience. It's crucial to recognize that experiencing these emotions is a part of the human experience. However, allowing them to dictate our actions and hinder our progress is a choice that can be challenged and changed.

To complement this understanding, let's draw inspiration from a quote by Eleanor Roosevelt:

"You gain strength, courage, and confidence by every experience in which you stop to look fear in the face. You must do the thing which you think you cannot do."

These words encapsulate the essence of confronting fear head-on and using it as a catalyst for personal growth. Moreover, doubt, when viewed as an opportunity for self-reflection and improvement, can be transformative.

As Henry Ford once said,

"Whether you think you can or you think

you can't, you're right."

This underscores the profound influence our beliefs have on our actions. By embracing a positive mindset and challenging self-limiting beliefs, we pave the way for overcoming doubt.

Chapter 2

THE PSYCHOLOGY BEHIND OVERTHINKING

Overthinking, the incessant analysis and reanalysis of situations can be a significant roadblock on the path to a clear and focused mind. In this chapter, we will delve into the intricate world of the psychology behind overthinking, exploring its roots, cognitive processes, and the profound impact it has on decision-making and overall well-being.

To comprehend overthinking, it's essential to recognize its origins. Often rooted in anxiety, fear of the unknown, or a desire for perfection, overthinking can manifest in various aspects of our lives. It's not merely a casual musing over choices but a relentless and often distressing mental activity that hampers our ability to make decisions and find satisfaction in them.

The cognitive processes contributing to overthinking are multifaceted. One key element is rumination – the repetitive dwelling on the same thoughts without resolving. Rumination not only intensifies negative emotions but also diverts cognitive resources from problem-solving to unproductive introspection.

Moreover, overthinking is closely linked to perfectionism, where individuals set unrealistically high standards for themselves. The constant pursuit of flawlessness can lead to a perpetual cycle of over-analysis, as every decision is weighed against an unattainable benchmark, amplifying stress and hindering progress.

To illustrate these concepts, let's consider the story of Alex, a young professional grappling with overthinking in his career. Faced with a myriad of choices, Alex found himself caught in a loop of indecision and self-doubt. His desire for the perfect outcome paralyzed him, highlighting the detrimental effects of overthinking on personal and professional development.

Understanding the impact of overthinking on decision-making is crucial. The excessive analysis that accompanies overthinking often leads to decision paralysis, where the fear of making the wrong choice prevents any choice at all. This not only impedes progress but can also result in missed opportunities and unfulfilled potential.

To address the psychology behind overthinking, it's beneficial to explore the concept of cognitive distortions. These distorted thought patterns, such as catastrophizing (expecting the worst outcome) and black-and-white thinking (seeing situations as all good or all bad), contribute to the amplification of worries and uncertainties, further fueling the overthinking cycle.

Breaking free from the chains of overthinking requires a multifaceted approach. Implementing mindfulness techniques can be instrumental in redirecting attention from rumination to the present moment. Mindfulness encourages awareness of thoughts without judgment, offering a valuable perspective to break the overthinking cycle.

Additionally, adopting a growth mindset, as popularized by psychologist Carol Dweck, can reshape our approach to challenges. Embracing setbacks as opportunities for learning and growth reduces the fear of making mistakes, mitigating the perfectionistic tendencies that fuel overthinking. As we navigate the complexities of overthinking, let's draw wisdom from the words of Mark Twain:

"I've had a lot of worries in my life, most of which never happened."

This quote encapsulates the futility of excessive worry and emphasizes the importance of breaking free from the shackles of overthinking.

Chapter 3

BUILDING MENTAL RESILIENCE

Mental resilience, the ability to bounce back from adversity and navigate life's challenges with strength and adaptability, is a cornerstone of a healthy and fulfilling existence. In this chapter, we embark on a profound exploration of strategies and practices aimed at building mental resilience. By understanding the components that contribute to resilience, we can equip ourselves with the tools needed to face life's uncertainties with grace and fortitude.

Understanding Resilience:

To embark on the journey of building mental resilience, it's essential to first grasp the concept itself. Resilience is not the absence of adversity but the capacity to respond effectively to life's challenges. It involves developing a mindset that views setbacks as opportunities for growth rather than insurmountable obstacles. Through resilience, individuals can weather storms, adapt to change, and emerge stronger on the other side.

The Components of Mental Resilience:

Building mental resilience involves nurturing various components that collectively contribute to a robust and adaptable mindset. One key aspect is emotional intelligence, the ability to understand and manage one's emotions effectively. Emotional intelligence allows individuals to navigate stress, maintain composure in challenging situations, and foster positive relationships. Another crucial component is self-efficacy, the belief in one's ability to overcome challenges and accomplish goals. Cultivating self-efficacy involves setting realistic goals, breaking them down into manageable steps, and celebrating small victories along the way. By fostering a sense of competence, individuals enhance their mental resilience.

Strategies for Cultivating Resilience:

1. Positive Thinking and Reframing: Resilient individuals often engage in positive thinking and reframing, viewing challenges as opportunities for growth. The power of reframing lies in shifting perspectives, turning obstacles into stepping stones.

2. Mindfulness and Stress Reduction: Incorporating mindfulness practices, such as meditation and deep breathing exercises, can significantly contribute to building mental resilience.

Mindfulness enhances self-awareness, reduces stress, and promotes a balanced perspective on life's challenges.

3. Social Support and Connection: Building a strong support network is a fundamental aspect of resilience. Meaningful connections with others provide emotional support, encouragement, and a sense of belonging. These relationships act as pillars during difficult times.

4. Adaptability and Flexibility: Resilient individuals exhibit adaptability and flexibility in the face of change. Embracing the idea that change is a constant and inevitable part of life fosters a mindset that is better equipped to navigate uncertainties.

To illustrate the transformative power of resilience, let's explore the journey of Maya, a single mother facing financial challenges and career uncertainties. Through the application of resilience strategies, Maya not only overcame adversity but also emerged with a renewed sense of purpose and determination.

The cultivation of mental resilience is an ongoing process that extends to daily life. Simple yet effective practices, such as maintaining a gratitude journal, setting realistic goals, and engaging in regular physical activity, contribute to the gradual strengthening of one's resilience. To inspire and reinforce the principles discussed, let's draw wisdom from notable figures:

- *"The human capacity for burden is like bamboo – far more flexible than you'd ever believe at first glance."* - Jodi Picoult

Chapter 4

REWIRING YOUR BRAIN FOR POSITIVITY

In the intricate landscape of the human mind, the power to reshape our thoughts and emotions is a profound tool for personal transformation. This chapter delves into the fascinating realm of neuroplasticity, exploring how we can actively rewire our brains for positivity. By understanding the science behind neuroplasticity and implementing practical techniques, individuals can cultivate a more positive and resilient mindset, fostering mental well-being.

Understanding Neuroplasticity:

Neuroplasticity is the brain's remarkable ability to reorganize itself by forming new neural connections throughout life. This concept challenges the traditional view that the brain's structure is fixed and unchangeable. The brain's plasticity allows it to adapt, learn, and rewire in response to experiences, thoughts, and behaviors.

The Impact of Positivity on the Brain:

Positive thoughts and emotions have a profound impact on the brain, influencing its structure and function. Studies in neuroscience have shown that positive experiences can stimulate the release of neurotransmitters such as dopamine and serotonin, contributing to feelings of happiness and well-being. By consciously fostering positivity, individuals can create a ripple effect that shapes the neural pathways associated with joy and resilience.

Practical Techniques for Positivity:

1. Positive Affirmations: The repetition of positive affirmations can create new neural pathways, reinforcing constructive beliefs and attitudes. Crafting personalized and meaningful affirmations and incorporating them into daily routines is a powerful technique for promoting positivity.

2. Gratitude Practices: Gratitude has been linked to increased activity in the brain's reward center. Engaging in regular gratitude practices, such as keeping a gratitude journal or expressing appreciation to others, can wire the brain to focus on the positive aspects of life.

3. Visualization and Imagery: The brain often struggles to differentiate between real and imagined experiences. Visualization exercises, where individuals vividly imagine positive scenarios and successful outcomes, can stimulate the brain in ways that mirror actual experiences, fostering a more optimistic outlook.

4. Acts of Kindness: Engaging in acts of kindness and generosity triggers the release of oxytocin, a neurotransmitter associated with social bonding and positive emotions. By incorporating small acts of kindness into daily life, individuals not only contribute to the well-being of others but also positively impact their brain chemistry.

Challenges and Overcoming Negativity Bias:

Despite the brain's plasticity, it has an inherent bias towards negativity—a survival mechanism designed to alert us to potential threats. Overcoming this negativity bias requires intentional effort. Strategies such as mindfulness meditation, which encourages non-judgmental awareness of thoughts, can help individuals observe negative patterns without being consumed by them.

Neuroplasticity in Action: Real-Life Stories:

Exploring real-life stories of individuals who actively rewired their brains for positivity provides concrete examples of the transformative power of neuroplasticity. From overcoming adversity to cultivating resilience, these stories showcase the profound impact of intentional brain rewiring. The journey of rewiring the brain for positivity extends beyond specific exercises. It involves integrating positive habits into daily life. From starting the day with a positive mindset to consciously choosing optimistic perspectives in challenging situations, these practices contribute to the gradual reshaping of neural pathways.

> *- "Your mind is like a parachute;*
>
> *it doesn't work if it's not open."*
>
> *- Frank Zappa*

Chapter 5

FACING AND CONQUERING FEARS

Fear, a primal emotion hardwired into our human psyche, has the power to paralyze and limit our potential. In this chapter, we embark on a profound exploration of facing and conquering fears. By understanding the nature of fear, identifying its manifestations, and implementing strategic approaches, we can transform fear from a hindrance into a catalyst for personal growth and empowerment.

Understanding the Nature of Fear:

Fear is a natural response designed to keep us safe in the face of perceived threats. However, in the complexities of modern life, fears often extend beyond immediate physical danger to encompass psychological and emotional challenges. Recognizing the multifaceted nature of fear is the first step toward conquering it. Fear can manifest in various forms, each presenting unique challenges. Common manifestations include the fear of failure, fear of rejection, fear of change, and fear of the unknown.

Unraveling the specific fears that hold us captive is crucial for developing targeted strategies to overcome them.

The Impact of Fear on Personal Growth:

While fear can provide a protective instinct, succumbing to irrational fears can stifle personal growth and limit our potential. Avoidance behaviors, procrastination, and self-sabotage often result from unaddressed fears. Confronting these fears head-on becomes a transformative journey toward self-discovery and empowerment. To conquer fears, it's essential to adopt a proactive mindset. Instead of allowing fears to dictate our actions, we can choose to face them consciously and deliberately. This shift in perspective is encapsulated in the words of Nelson Mandela:

> *"I learned that courage was not the absence of fear, but the triumph over it. The brave man is not he who does not feel afraid, but he who conquers that fear."*

Gradual Exposure Therapy:

One effective strategy for facing fears is gradual exposure therapy. This approach involves progressively exposing oneself to the feared situation or stimulus in a controlled and supportive manner. Gradual exposure allows individuals to build resilience and diminish the intensity of fear responses over time.

To illustrate the power of gradual exposure therapy, consider the story of Emily, who battled a paralyzing fear of public speaking. Through a step-by-step approach, starting with small and manageable speaking engagements, Emily gradually expanded her comfort zone, ultimately conquering her fear and discovering newfound confidence. Throughout history, individuals have triumphed over profound fears, leaving a legacy of inspiration. Examining the stories of figures like Eleanor Roosevelt, who overcame the fear of public scrutiny to become a powerful advocate for human rights, reinforces the notion that fear can be a stepping stone to greatness when faced courageously. Building resilience becomes paramount in the face of fear. Resilience involves developing coping mechanisms and the ability to bounce back from setbacks. Strategies such as positive affirmations, mindfulness, and seeking support from a network of friends or mentors contribute to the cultivation of resilience in navigating fearful situations.

Overcoming Fear of Failure:

The fear of failure is a pervasive and potent force that often holds individuals back from pursuing their goals. By reframing the concept of failure as a learning opportunity, setting realistic expectations, and embracing a growth mindset, individuals can diminish the paralyzing impact of this fear and forge ahead on their path to success.

Conquering Fear:

Drawing inspiration from individuals who faced and conquered their fears reinforces the potential for triumph:

- "I must not fear. Fear is the mind-killer. Fear is the little death that brings total obliteration." - Frank Herbert, Dune

Chapter 6

DEVELOPING A GROWTH MINDSET

The Impact of Social Comparisons on Mindset:

Social comparisons, a common aspect of human interaction, can significantly influence mindset. Individuals with a growth mindset view others' successes not as threats to their worth but as opportunities to learn and grow. By shifting the focus from competition to collaboration, a growth mindset fosters a supportive and encouraging social environment.

Neuroscience of a Growth Mindset:

Recent studies in neuroscience have shed light on the physical changes that occur in the brain when adopting a growth mindset. Neuroplasticity, the brain's ability to reorganize itself, is heightened when individuals engage in activities that challenge them and stimulate learning. This biological aspect underscores the validity and transformative potential of cultivating a growth mindset.

<u>APPLYING A GROWTH MINDSET TO SPECIFIC DOMAINS:</u>

1. Education: In educational settings, cultivating a growth mindset among students can lead to improved learning outcomes. Teachers can foster this mindset by praising effort and persistence, providing constructive feedback, and creating an environment that encourages curiosity and exploration.

2. Workplace: A growth mindset is a catalyst for innovation and adaptability in the workplace. Companies that prioritize continuous learning, encourage risk-taking, and provide opportunities for skill development create a culture where employees can thrive and contribute to the organization's success.

3. Relationships: Applying a growth mindset to relationships involves recognizing that individuals and dynamics can evolve over time. Embracing challenges, communicating openly, and learning from relationship experiences contribute to personal growth and the development of stronger, more resilient connections.

4. Personal Goals: Whether pursuing fitness, creative endeavors, or other personal goals, a growth mindset is instrumental in overcoming obstacles. Setting realistic goals, persisting through challenges, and celebrating small victories contribute to a positive and forward-thinking approach.

CHALLENGES IN CULTIVATING A GROWTH MINDSET:

While the benefits of a growth mindset are clear, the process of cultivating this mindset comes with its own set of challenges. Overcoming deeply ingrained fixed mindset tendencies, addressing self-doubt, and navigating societal pressures require intentional effort and a commitment to continuous self-improvement. Positive affirmations, already explored in the context of rewiring the brain for positivity, play a crucial role in developing a growth mindset. Affirmations that reinforce the belief in one's capacity for learning, resilience, and improvement become powerful tools for transforming mindset over time.

INTERACTIVE EXERCISES FOR DEVELOPING A GROWTH MINDSET:

1. Mindset Journaling: Keeping a mindset journal allows individuals to track their thoughts, challenges, and progress. Reflecting on experiences, identifying fixed mindset tendencies, and reframing them into growth-oriented perspectives contribute to mindset transformation.

2. Goal Setting Workshop: Hosting a goal-setting workshop, either individually or in a group setting, encourages individuals to define their aspirations, break them down into manageable steps, and commit to consistent effort. This interactive exercise reinforces the principles of a growth mindset in the context of personal development.

3. Peer-to-Peer Learning Circles: Creating peer-to-peer learning circles promotes a collaborative environment where individuals share their experiences, challenges, and strategies for adopting a growth mindset. Learning from others' journeys enhances collective motivation and reinforces the belief in the transformative power of continuous learning.

Quotations on Lifelong Learning and Growth:

Inspiring quotes that underscore the importance of lifelong learning and growth:

- *"The more that you read, the more things you will know. The more that you learn, the more places you'll go." - Dr. Seuss*

- *"Anyone who stops learning is old, whether at twenty or eighty. Anyone who keeps learning stays young." - Henry Ford*

Chapter 7

PRACTICAL STRATEGIES TO HALT OVERTHINKING

Overthinking, the incessant and often debilitating process of dwelling on thoughts and scenarios, can hinder decision-making, increase stress, and impede overall well-being. This chapter delves into practical strategies to halt overthinking, offering a comprehensive guide for individuals seeking to break free from the cycle of excessive rumination and foster a more focused and balanced mental state.

UNDERSTANDING OVERTHINKING:

Before delving into strategies to halt overthinking, it's crucial to understand its roots and manifestations. Overthinking often stems from a variety of factors, including anxiety, fear of making the wrong decision, perfectionism, and a tendency to ruminate on past events. Recognizing the triggers and cognitive patterns associated with overthinking is the first step toward effective intervention. Overthinking can have profound implications for mental health, contributing to heightened stress, anxiety disorders, and even depression. The continuous loop of intrusive thoughts and the inability to make decisions can create a cycle of negative emotions, eroding overall well-being. Addressing overthinking is not only a quest for mental clarity but also a proactive step toward preserving and enhancing mental health. Mindfulness, the practice of being fully present in the moment without judgment, serves as a powerful antidote to overthinking. Cultivating mindfulness involves a range of techniques, including meditation, deep breathing exercises, and sensory awareness. Integrating mindfulness into daily life disrupts the overthinking cycle by redirecting focus to the present, fostering a sense of calm and clarity.

1. MINDFUL BREATHING EXERCISES:

- Diaphragmatic Breathing: Engaging in diaphragmatic breathing, also known as deep belly breathing, promotes relaxation and reduces stress. Individuals can practice this by inhaling deeply through the nose, allowing the diaphragm to expand, and exhaling slowly through pursed lips.

- 4-7-8 Breathing Technique: This technique involves inhaling for a count of 4, holding the breath for a count of 7, and exhaling for a count of 8. The rhythmic nature of this exercise induces a calming effect, interrupting the overthinking cycle.

2. Body Scan Meditation:

   - Guided body scan meditations encourage individuals to focus attention on different parts of the body, progressively releasing tension and promoting relaxation. This mindful practice heightens awareness of bodily sensations, diverting attention from overthinking.

3. Grounding Techniques:

   - Grounding techniques involve connecting with the present moment through sensory experiences. For example, individuals can focus on the sensation of their feet on the ground, the texture of an object, or the taste of a food item. This sensory engagement interrupts overthinking by anchoring attention to the immediate surroundings.

STRATEGIES FOR BREAKING COGNITIVE PATTERNS:

Overthinking often involves negative thought patterns that perpetuate anxiety and indecision. Intervening in these cognitive patterns is essential for halting overthinking and fostering a more constructive mindset.

1. Cognitive Restructuring:

  - Cognitive restructuring involves identifying and challenging irrational or negative thoughts. By questioning the validity of these thoughts and replacing them with more balanced and realistic alternatives, individuals can reshape their cognitive patterns and reduce overthinking.

2. Mindful Self-Compassion:

  - Developing a compassionate attitude toward oneself is integral to breaking negative thought patterns associated with overthinking. Practicing self-compassion involves treating oneself with kindness and understanding, and acknowledging that everyone makes mistakes and faces challenges.

3. The ABCD Model:

  - The ABCD model stands for Adversity, Beliefs, Consequences, and Disputation. This cognitive-behavioral technique encourages individuals to identify the Adversity (trigger), examine their Beliefs about the situation, explore the Consequences (emotional and behavioral), and engage in Disputation by challenging and reframing unhelpful beliefs.

STRATEGIES FOR DECISION-MAKING:

Overthinking often revolves around indecision and fear of making the wrong choice. Implementing effective decision-making strategies can alleviate the mental burden associated with overthinking.

1. Pros and Cons Analysis:

  - Conducting a pros and cons analysis involves listing the advantages and disadvantages of a decision. This structured approach provides a visual representation of the potential outcomes, aiding individuals in making informed choices and reducing overthinking.

2. Setting Decision-Making Criteria:

  - Establishing clear criteria for decision-making helps individuals prioritize factors that are most important to them. By aligning choices with predetermined criteria, individuals can streamline the decision-making process and mitigate overthinking.

3. Implementing a Time Limit:

  - Overthinking often thrives in an environment of endless rumination. Setting a specific time limit for decision-making forces individuals to focus on key considerations, preventing excessive analysis and breaking the cycle of overthinking.

<u>**CREATING A SUPPORTIVE ENVIRONMENT:**</u>

The environment in which individuals navigate their daily lives can significantly influence overthinking tendencies. Establishing a supportive and conducive environment fosters mental well-being and provides a foundation for breaking free from overthinking.

1. Mindful Environment Design:

   - Creating a mindful environment involves minimizing distractions, organizing spaces, and incorporating elements that promote relaxation. A clutter-free and aesthetically pleasing environment contributes to mental clarity and reduces overthinking triggers.

2. Establishing Healthy Routines:

   - Consistent routines provide a sense of structure and predictability, reducing the likelihood of overthinking. Establishing healthy habits, such as regular exercise, sufficient sleep, and balanced nutrition, contributes to overall well-being and resilience against overthinking.

3. Seeking Social Support:

   - Sharing concerns and thoughts with trusted friends, family members, or mentors can provide valuable perspectives and emotional support. Social connections act as a buffer against

overthinking, offering alternative viewpoints, and fostering a
sense of belonging.

STRATEGIES FOR PRACTICING ACCEPTANCE:

Overthinking often involves resistance to uncertainty and a
desire for control. Embracing acceptance-oriented strategies
can help individuals navigate ambiguity and reduce the
compulsion to overanalyze.

1 Mindful Acceptance:

  - Mindful acceptance involves acknowledging and allowing
thoughts and emotions without judgment. Instead of resisting
or suppressing thoughts, individuals practice observing them
with curiosity and detachment. This approach diminishes the
intensity of overthinking.

2. Letting Go of Control:

  - Accepting that not everything is within one's control is a
crucial aspect of halting overthinking. Letting go of the need for
certainty and embracing the unpredictability of life contributes
to a more adaptable mindset.

3. Mindfulness-Based Stress Reduction (MBSR):

   - MBSR, developed by Jon Kabat-Zinn, integrates mindfulness meditation and awareness techniques to reduce stress and enhance well-being. This structured program incorporates mindfulness practices to cultivate acceptance and mitigate overthinking.

COMBINING STRATEGIES FOR HOLISTIC OVERTHINKING PREVENTION:

Effectively halting overthinking often involves integrating multiple strategies that address various aspects of cognitive patterns, decision-making, environmental influences, and acceptance. Combining these strategies creates a holistic approach to overthinking prevention.

1. Mindful Decision-Making Framework:

   - A mindful decision-making framework combines elements of mindfulness with structured decision-making techniques. By approaching decisions with a calm and present mindset, individuals can mitigate overthinking while making choices aligned with their values.

2. The 5-Step Overthinking Intervention:

   - This intervention involves:

a. Identifying Overthinking Patterns: Recognizing triggers and cognitive patterns.

   b. Engaging in Mindful Techniques: Practicing mindfulness exercises to redirect focus.

   c. Applying Decision-Making Strategies: Utilizing decision-making techniques.

   d. Creating Supportive Environments: Establishing conducive surroundings.

   e. Practicing Acceptance: Embracing acceptance-oriented strategies.

OVERCOMING OVERTHINKING CHALLENGES

While implementing strategies to halt overthinking, individuals may encounter challenges such as setbacks, resistance to change, or difficulty in maintaining consistent practices. Addressing these challenges involves a combination of self-awareness, resilience-building, and ongoing commitment to personal growth.

1. Resilience-Building Exercises:

  - Engaging in resilience-building exercises, such as goal-setting, positive affirmations, and seeking social support during challenging times, strengthens individuals' ability to navigate setbacks and persist in their efforts to halt overthinking.

2. Cognitive Behavioral Therapy (CBT):

   - CBT, a therapeutic approach, offers structured interventions for addressing overthinking. By working with a qualified therapist, individuals can explore the roots of overthinking, challenge irrational thoughts, and develop coping strategies to promote lasting change.

REAL-LIFE OVERTHINKING STORIES:

Exploring the personal journeys of individuals who successfully halted overthinking provides inspiration and practical insights. These stories illustrate the transformative power of implementing strategies and offer relatable examples of overcoming the challenges associated with overthinking.

1. Anna's Journey to Decision-Making Clarity:

   - Anna, a professional facing a career crossroads, struggled with overthinking and indecision. By incorporating mindfulness practices, setting decision-making criteria, and seeking mentorship, Anna navigated the complexity of her choices and emerged with a newfound sense of clarity and confidence.

2. James' Path to Breaking Negative Thought Patterns:

- James, grappling with chronic overthinking and self-doubt, implemented cognitive restructuring techniques and engaged in self-compassion practices. Through consistent effort and a commitment to challenging negative thought patterns, James transformed his mindset and cultivated a more positive and resilient outlook.

- "Overthinking ruins you. It ruins the situation, twists it around, makes you worry, and just makes everything much worse than it actually is." - Unknown

Chapter 8

NURTURING SELF-ESTEEM AND CONFIDENCE

- "Confidence comes not from always being right, but from not fearing to be wrong."

- Peter T. McIntyre

Nurturing a Positive Self-Image:

Self-esteem and confidence are foundational elements of a fulfilling and empowered life. This chapter explores the intricacies of nurturing a positive self-image, providing practical strategies to enhance self-esteem and cultivate unwavering confidence. Understanding the dynamics of self-esteem, addressing common challenges, and implementing effective practices are key components of this transformative journey. At the core of self-esteem lies the perception we hold about ourselves — our worth, abilities, and inherent value. Developing a deep understanding of the foundations of self-esteem is essential for fostering a positive self-image and building lasting confidence.

1. Self-Reflection for Self-Understanding:

   - Engaging in self-reflection involves exploring personal beliefs, values, and experiences that shape self-perception. By delving into the roots of self-esteem, individuals gain insights into the factors that contribute to their self-image, paving the way for targeted interventions and positive transformations.

2. The Role of Childhood and Early Experiences:

   - Childhood experiences play a pivotal role in shaping self-esteem. Positive affirmations, encouragement, and a supportive environment during formative years contribute to a healthy self-image. Conversely, negative experiences or criticism can leave lasting imprints, requiring conscious efforts to reframe and rebuild self-esteem.

3. The Connection Between Self-Compassion and Self-Esteem:

   - Self-compassion, the practice of treating oneself with kindness and understanding, forms a symbiotic relationship with self-esteem. Cultivating self-compassion involves acknowledging imperfections without judgment, fostering a nurturing inner dialogue, and embracing one's humanity. This compassionate approach becomes a powerful catalyst for enhancing self-esteem.

4. External Validation vs. Intrinsic Value:

- Distinguishing between seeking external validation and recognizing intrinsic value is integral to building a robust self-esteem foundation. While external validation can provide temporary boosts, relying solely on external approval is unsustainable. Cultivating a sense of intrinsic value involves recognizing one's worth independent of external opinions.

ADDRESSING COMMON CHALLENGES TO SELF-ESTEEM:

Challenges to self-esteem are ubiquitous, ranging from societal pressures and comparison to unrealistic standards, to inner self-criticism and imposter syndrome. Identifying and addressing these common challenges is crucial for nurturing a positive self-image.

1. Coping with Societal Pressures:

- Societal expectations and standards often contribute to feelings of inadequacy. Addressing societal pressures involves cultivating self-awareness, questioning unrealistic ideals, and consciously choosing paths aligned with personal values rather than societal norms.

2. Navigating Comparison and Envy:

 - The prevalence of social media intensifies the culture of comparison and envy. Navigating these challenges requires cultivating gratitude, appreciating individual uniqueness, and recognizing that everyone's journey is distinct. Focusing on personal growth and achievements rather than external benchmarks becomes instrumental in maintaining a positive self-image.

3. Overcoming Inner Self-Criticism:

 - Inner self-criticism, the relentless voice of self-doubt and negativity, is a significant obstacle to self-esteem. Overcoming this challenge involves developing self-awareness, challenging negative thoughts, and practicing self-compassion. Implementing positive affirmations and reframing self-talk contribute to building a more supportive inner dialogue.

4. Addressing Imposter Syndrome:

 - Imposter syndrome, the belief that one's accomplishments are undeserved and the fear of being exposed as a fraud, undermines confidence and self-esteem. Addressing imposter syndrome involves acknowledging achievements, recognizing competence, and reframing perfectionist tendencies. Sharing experiences with others who face similar challenges can also provide reassurance and validation.

<u>**BUILDING CONFIDENCE THROUGH ACTION AND ACHIEVEMENT:**</u>

Confidence is a dynamic quality cultivated through intentional action and the accumulation of achievements. This section

explores strategies for building confidence, embracing challenges, and fostering a resilient mindset that withstands setbacks.

1. Setting and Achieving Realistic Goals:

  - Setting realistic and achievable goals is a foundational step in building confidence. Break down larger goals into manageable steps, celebrate small victories, and gradually increase the complexity of challenges. The process of setting and attaining goals reinforces a sense of capability and fosters confidence.

2. The Power of Positive Visualization:

  - Positive visualization involves mentally rehearsing successful outcomes and envisioning oneself confidently navigating challenges. This technique harnesses the mind's ability to influence behavior, preparing individuals for success and boosting confidence. Regular practice of positive visualization contributes to a more optimistic and empowered mindset.

3. Embracing a Growth Mindset:

- Adopting a growth mindset, explored in a previous chapter, is pivotal for building confidence. Embracing challenges as opportunities for learning and viewing setbacks as stepping stones to improvement cultivates resilience and a belief in one's capacity for growth. Individuals with a growth mindset approach new endeavors with enthusiasm and a willingness to learn from experiences.

4. Expanding Comfort Zones:

- Confidence flourishes when individuals step outside their comfort zones. Actively seeking growth opportunities, whether in professional, social, or personal realms, exposes individuals to new challenges and experiences. Each successful venture beyond the comfort zone contributes to an expanding sense of confidence.

FOSTERING POSITIVE SELF-TALK AND AFFIRMATIONS:

The language individuals use when speaking to themselves has a profound impact on self-esteem and confidence. Fostering positive self-talk and incorporating affirmations into daily routines reinforces a constructive and supportive internal dialogue.

1. Identifying and Challenging Negative Self-Talk:

- Identifying negative self-talk involves paying attention to recurring thoughts that undermine confidence. Challenging these thoughts by questioning their validity, reframing them in a more positive light, and consciously choosing empowering language contribute to cultivating a positive internal dialogue.

2. Crafting Personalized Positive Affirmations:

- Personalized positive affirmations serve as powerful tools for building confidence. Crafting affirmations that reflect individual strengths, aspirations, and values creates a personalized roadmap to bolster self-esteem. Regular repetition of these affirmations reinforces positive beliefs and contributes to a resilient mindset.

3. Affirmation Journaling:

- Affirmation journaling involves recording positive affirmations, reflections on achievements, and expressions of self-gratitude. This practice not only serves as a tangible record of accomplishments but also becomes a source of inspiration during challenging times. Regularly revisiting the affirmation journal reinforces positive self-perception.

Creating a Supportive Social Network:

The impact of social interactions on self-esteem and confidence is profound. Building and maintaining a supportive social network contributes to a positive self-image, provides validation, and offers encouragement during challenging times.

1. Surrounding Oneself with Positive Influences:

 - Actively choosing to surround oneself with positive influences and supportive individuals is a proactive step in nurturing self-esteem. Cultivating relationships with people who celebrate achievements, provide constructive feedback, and offer encouragement creates a foundation for confidence-building.

2. Seeking Constructive Feedback:

 - Seeking feedback, both positive and constructive, from trusted individuals fosters personal and professional growth. Constructive feedback provides valuable insights, highlights areas for improvement, and contributes to a more accurate and balanced self-perception. Embracing feedback as a tool for refinement strengthens confidence.

OVERCOMING **S**ETBACKS AND **B**UILDING **R**ESILIENCE:

Setbacks are inevitable in the pursuit of personal and professional growth. Overcoming setbacks and building resilience are integral components of nurturing self-esteem and confidence. This section explores strategies for navigating challenges and bouncing back from adversity.

1. Learning from Setbacks:

   - Viewing setbacks as opportunities for learning is a transformative mindset shift. Instead of interpreting failures as reflections of incompetence, individuals can extract valuable lessons, identify areas for improvement, and use setbacks as springboards for future success.

2. Cultivating Resilience:

   - Resilience, the ability to bounce back from adversity, is a key attribute in maintaining confidence. Cultivating resilience involves developing coping mechanisms, fostering a positive mindset, and acknowledging the inherent capacity to overcome challenges. Resilient individuals view setbacks as temporary hurdles rather than insurmountable obstacles.

Celebrating Personal Achievements:

Celebrating personal achievements, regardless of their scale, is a fundamental aspect of nurturing self-esteem and confidence. Recognizing and acknowledging one's successes, both big and small, contributes to a positive self-image and reinforces the belief in one's abilities.

1. Creating a Success Journal:

- A success journal serves as a repository for recording personal achievements, milestones, and moments of triumph. Regularly updating the success journal provides a visual reminder of individual capabilities and serves as a source of motivation during challenging times.

2. Reflecting on Growth and Progress:

   - Reflecting on personal growth and progress involves acknowledging the distance traveled on one's journey. Whether in professional development, skill acquisition, or personal goals, recognizing incremental progress contributes to a sense of accomplishment and reinforces confidence in one's abilities.

REAL-LIFE CONFIDENCE-BUILDING STORIES:

Exploring real-life stories of individuals who embarked on journeys to nurture self-esteem and build confidence offers tangible examples of transformation and resilience. These stories showcase the diversity of paths and strategies employed to overcome challenges and foster self-assurance.

1. Emma's Odyssey to Self-Discovery:

   - Emma, facing self-doubt and uncertainty, embarked on a journey of self-discovery. Through self-reflection, positive visualization, and surrounding herself with supportive influences, Emma gradually built confidence and embraced her unique qualities. Her story underscores the transformative power of intentional self-care and belief in one's capabilities.

2. John's Path to Resilience after Setbacks:

  - John encountered setbacks in his professional endeavors, leading to a dip in confidence. Through learning from setbacks, seeking constructive feedback, and cultivating resilience, John not only overcame challenges but also emerged with a heightened sense of self-assurance. His journey illustrates the resilience-building process and the transformative potential of setbacks.

Chapter 9:

OVERCOMING DOUBT IN DECISIONMAKING

In the intricate tapestry of life, decision-making serves as a vital thread weaving through various aspects of our personal and professional spheres. However, this process is not immune to the pervasive influence of doubt. Doubt, a natural and universal human experience, can manifest as uncertainty, hesitation, and anxiety, potentially hindering effective decision-making. This chapter explores the multifaceted nature of doubt in decision-making and provides a comprehensive guide to overcoming its challenges. From understanding the psychology of doubt to implementing practical strategies for confident decision-making, this exploration aims to empower individuals on their journey towards making sound and decisive choices.

UNDERSTANDING THE PSYCHOLOGY OF DOUBT:

Doubt, often viewed as a negative force, is an inherent aspect of the human psyche. It stems from a combination of factors, including fear of making the wrong decision, uncertainty about the future, and a desire for control. Recognizing the psychological underpinnings of doubt is the first step in dismantling its barriers to effective decision-making. Psychologists posit that doubt can be categorized into different forms, such as self-doubt, situational doubt, and decision-specific doubt. Self-doubt involves questioning one's abilities and worthiness, situational doubt arises from external uncertainties, and decision-specific doubt emerges when faced with a particular choice. Understanding these nuances allows individuals to pinpoint the root causes of their doubt, facilitating targeted interventions.

THE IMPACT OF DOUBT ON DECISION-MAKING:

Doubt, when left unaddressed, can exert a profound impact on the decision-making process. It can lead to decision paralysis, where individuals find themselves unable to commit to a choice due to fear of negative outcomes. The emotional toll of doubt can manifest as stress, anxiety, and a pervasive sense of unease, creating a barrier to clear and rational decision-making.

Moreover, doubt can contribute to second-guessing, where individuals continuously question and reevaluate their decisions even after they have been made. This cycle of doubt perpetuates a lack of confidence in one's choices and undermines the ability to trust one's judgment. Understanding the repercussions of doubt on decision-making underscores the urgency of developing strategies to overcome its influence.

STRATEGIES FOR OVERCOMING DOUBT:

Overcoming doubt in decision-making involves a combination of self-awareness, cognitive reframing, and proactive strategies. The goal is not to eliminate doubt entirely, as it is a natural aspect of the human experience, but rather to navigate it constructively and mitigate its impact on decision-making. The following strategies offer a roadmap for individuals seeking to cultivate confidence and decisiveness in their choices.

1. Cultivating Self-Awareness:

Developing self-awareness involves recognizing the patterns of doubt that arise in different decision-making scenarios. By pinpointing specific triggers and thought processes associated with doubt, individuals can proactively address these challenges. Mindfulness practices, such as meditation and reflective journaling, serve as effective tools for enhancing self-awareness.

2. Challenging Negative Thought Patterns:

Doubt often accompanies negative thought patterns, such as catastrophic thinking, overgeneralization, and all-or-nothing thinking. Challenging these patterns involves questioning the validity of negative thoughts, seeking evidence to the contrary, and reframing them in a more balanced and realistic light. Cognitive-behavioral techniques are instrumental in this process.

3. Building Decision-Making Competence:

Confidence in decision-making is closely linked to competence. Building decision-making competence involves acquiring relevant information, honing critical thinking skills, and seeking expertise when needed. By enhancing decision-making abilities, individuals can bolster their confidence and trust in the choices they make.

4. Embracing a Growth Mindset:

A growth mindset, explored in earlier chapters, plays a crucial role in overcoming doubt. Embracing challenges as opportunities for learning and viewing decisions as avenues for growth shift the perspective from a fixed mindset to one of continuous development. This mindset fosters resilience and adaptability in the face of uncertainty.

5. Setting Realistic Expectations:

Unrealistic expectations contribute to doubt by creating a standard of perfection that is unattainable. Setting realistic expectations involves acknowledging that no decision is flawless and that mistakes are a natural part of the learning process. Accepting the imperfections inherent in decision-making cultivates a more forgiving and confident approach.

6. Implementing Decision-Making Frameworks:

Decision-making frameworks provide structured approaches to choices, reducing the complexity and ambiguity that often fuel doubt. Techniques such as pros and cons analysis, decision trees, and SWOT analysis offer systematic ways to evaluate options and make informed decisions. Having a clear process in place enhances confidence in the decision-making journey.

7. Consulting Trusted Advisors:

Seeking advice from trusted advisors, mentors, or peers can offer valuable perspectives and insights. Consulting others not only provides diverse viewpoints but also instills a sense of reassurance and support. Trusted advisors serve as sounding boards and contribute to the decision-making process by offering guidance based on their experiences and expertise.

8. Emotional Regulation Techniques:

Doubt often triggers emotional responses that can cloud judgment. Emotional regulation techniques, such as deep breathing exercises, mindfulness meditation, and progressive muscle relaxation, help individuals manage anxiety and stress associated with decision-making. By fostering emotional resilience, individuals can approach choices with a clearer and calmer mindset.

REAL-LIFE DECISION-MAKING STORIES:

Exploring real-life decision-making stories offers tangible examples of individuals overcoming doubt and making confident choices.

1. Sarah's Career Crossroads:

Sarah faced a pivotal career decision that evoked self-doubt and uncertainty. Through self-awareness practices, consultation with mentors, and setting realistic expectations, Sarah navigated the decision-making process with confidence. Her story illustrates the transformative power of combining internal reflection with external guidance.

2. Alex's Entrepreneurial Venture:

Alex embarked on an entrepreneurial venture that brought forth doubts about the viability of his business idea. By embracing a growth mindset, seeking advice from industry experts, and implementing decision-making frameworks, Alex not only launched a successful venture but also developed newfound confidence in his entrepreneurial abilities.

- "Trust yourself. Think for yourself. Act for yourself. Speak for yourself. Be yourself. Imitation is suicide."

- Marva Collins

Chapter 10

EMBRACING FAILURE AS A STEPPING STONE

"I have not failed. I've just found 10,000 ways that won't work."

- Thomas A. Edison

In the intricate tapestry of personal and professional growth, the concept of failure often emerges as a formidable adversary. However, this chapter seeks to redefine failure as a valuable and transformative stepping stone on the path to success. From understanding the psychology of failure to embracing resilience-building strategies, we will explore how individuals can navigate setbacks, extract lessons, and use failure as a catalyst for future achievements.

UNDERSTANDING THE PSYCHOLOGY OF FAILURE:

1. The Perception of Failure:

The perception of failure is subjective and deeply ingrained in societal norms and personal beliefs. Shifting the lens through which failure is viewed, from a negative judgment to a neutral or even positive learning experience, forms the foundation for embracing failure as a stepping stone.

2. Cognitive Appraisal of Failure:

Cognitive appraisal plays a crucial role in how individuals respond to failure. Examining the thoughts and beliefs associated with failure allows for a more nuanced understanding. By challenging distorted thinking patterns and reframing failure as a temporary setback rather than a permanent defeat, individuals can cultivate a resilient mindset.

3. Fear of Failure:

The fear of failure can be a paralyzing force, hindering individuals from taking risks and pursuing their goals. Understanding the roots of this fear, whether rooted in perfectionism, societal expectations, or past experiences, is essential for dismantling its hold and embracing failure as a natural part of the learning process.

THE TRANSFORMATIVE POWER OF FAILURE:

1. Failure as a Source of Learning:

Failure provides a rich source of learning that cannot be replicated through success alone. Analyzing the factors that led to failure, identifying areas for improvement, and extracting valuable lessons contribute to personal and professional growth. Failure becomes a teacher, offering insights that success might not reveal.

2. Building Resilience through Setbacks:

Resilience, the ability to bounce back from adversity, is a key byproduct of navigating failure. Each setback offers an opportunity to develop resilience by facing challenges head-on, adapting to change, and learning to persevere in the face of obstacles. Embracing failure as a stepping stone reinforces mental fortitude.

3. Cultivating a Growth Mindset:

A growth mindset involves viewing challenges, including failure, as opportunities for learning and development. Embracing a growth mindset means recognizing that abilities can be cultivated over time through effort and dedication. This mindset shift transforms failure from a reflection of inadequacy to a springboard for improvement.

STRATEGIES FOR EMBRACING FAILURE:

1. Mindful Reflection after Failure:

Mindful reflection involves objectively examining the circumstances surrounding failure without self-judgment. This practice allows individuals to gain clarity on contributing factors, identify areas for improvement, and extract meaningful insights. Mindful reflection fosters a constructive approach to failure.

2. Setting Realistic Expectations:

Unrealistic expectations can magnify the impact of failure. Setting realistic expectations involves acknowledging that setbacks are a natural part of any journey and do not define one's worth or capabilities. By embracing the inevitability of failure, individuals can approach challenges with a healthier perspective.

3. Fostering Self-Compassion:

Self-compassion is a crucial component of embracing failure. Treating oneself with kindness, acknowledging the emotional toll of setbacks, and refraining from harsh self-criticism create a supportive internal environment. Self-compassion acts as a buffer against the emotional aftermath of failure.

4. Building a Support System:

A strong support system provides solace and encouragement during times of failure. Sharing experiences with trusted friends, family, or mentors creates a sense of connection and perspective. Constructive feedback and emotional support from others contribute to a more resilient response to failure.

5. Understanding the Role of Perseverance:

Perseverance, the commitment to persist in the face of challenges, is integral to embracing failure as a stepping stone. Recognizing that success often involves overcoming multiple failures requires a steadfast determination to continue pursuing goals despite setbacks. Perseverance transforms failure into a temporary detour rather than a roadblock.

6. Celebrating Small Wins:

Celebrating small wins, even in the midst of failure, contributes to a positive mindset. Recognizing and acknowledging incremental progress, no matter how minor, reinforces a sense of achievement. Small victories serve as reminders that failure is not an all-encompassing defeat but rather a part of a larger journey.

<u>REAL-LIFE STORIES OF EMBRACING FAILURE:</u>

1. Samantha's Entrepreneurial Journey:

   Samantha's initial venture faced unexpected challenges and setbacks. Rather than viewing failure as a roadblock, she embraced it as an invaluable learning experience. Through mindful reflection, adjustments to her business strategy, and unwavering perseverance, Samantha transformed initial failures into the stepping stones that led to a successful entrepreneurial career.

2. Robert's Professional Growth through Setbacks:

   Robert navigated professional setbacks that initially seemed insurmountable. By fostering self-compassion, seeking guidance from mentors, and leveraging failure as an opportunity to reassess and recalibrate, he not only rebounded but also experienced substantial personal and career growth. Robert's story illustrates the transformative power of embracing failure with resilience.

1. Shifting Cultural Narratives:

Societal attitudes towards failure often contribute to the fear and stigma surrounding setbacks. Shifting cultural narratives involves challenging the notion that failure equates to incompetence and reframing it as a normal part of the human experience. By promoting a more compassionate and understanding view of failure, societal pressures can be alleviated.

2. Encouraging a Growth Mindset in Education:

Educational institutions play a significant role in shaping attitudes towards failure. Encouraging a growth mindset in education involves fostering an environment where mistakes are viewed as opportunities for learning. Incorporating failure as a natural aspect of the learning process helps students develop resilience and adaptability.

3. Redefining Success Beyond Achievements:

Redefining success beyond external achievements involves acknowledging the holistic nature of personal and professional growth. Emphasizing qualities such as resilience, adaptability, and a willingness to learn as integral components of success helps individuals detach from narrow definitions and embrace the inherent value of failure in the broader context of life's journey.

"Failure is not the opposite of success; it's part of success." - Arianna Huffington

Chapter 11

TRANSFORMING DOUBT INTO MOTIVATION

Doubt, often viewed as a hindrance, has the transformative potential to become a powerful source of motivation. This chapter explores the dynamics of doubt, understanding its origins, and providing practical strategies to harness doubt's energy for positive change. From reframing self-doubt to leveraging uncertainty as a catalyst for growth, individuals can transform doubt into a driving force on their journey toward personal and professional fulfillment.

"Doubt kills more dreams than failure ever will."

- Suzy Kassem

<u>UNDERSTANDING THE NATURE OF DOUBT:</u>

1. Exploring the Psychology of Doubt:

Doubt is a complex emotion rooted in fear, uncertainty, and a lack of confidence. Understanding the psychological underpinnings of doubt involves delving into its cognitive and emotional aspects. By recognizing doubt as a natural response to challenges, individuals can reframe their perception and unlock their motivational potential.

2. Identifying Types of Doubt:

Doubt manifests in various forms, including self-doubt, situational doubt, and doubt about decisions. Recognizing the specific type of doubt individuals experience allows for targeted interventions. Whether doubting one's abilities, the outcome of a situation, or the validity of a decision, each form presents an opportunity for transformation.

3. The Impact of Doubt on Motivation:

Doubt, when left unaddressed, can dampen motivation and hinder progress. However, when channeled constructively, doubt can serve as a powerful motivator. This chapter explores the delicate balance between doubt's potential to paralyze and its capacity to ignite a fire within individuals, propelling them towards achieving their goals.

<u>TRANSFORMATIVE STRATEGIES FOR DOUBT:</u>

1. Reframing Self-Doubt:

   Self-doubt often stems from negative self-perceptions and limiting beliefs. Reframing self-doubt involves challenging these negative thoughts, recognizing achievements and strengths, and cultivating a positive self-image. By reframing self-doubt as an indicator of areas for growth rather than a sign of incompetence, individuals can turn it into a motivational ally.

2. Setting Incremental Goals:

Doubt can be overwhelming when faced with lofty objectives. Breaking down larger goals into smaller, achievable milestones provides a roadmap for success. Setting incremental goals not only makes the journey more manageable but also allows individuals to celebrate victories along the way, reinforcing their motivation to overcome doubt.

3. Learning from Past Doubt-Driven Success:

Reflecting on past instances where doubt fueled motivation and led to success provides valuable insights. Analyzing these experiences allows individuals to identify patterns, strengths, and coping mechanisms that proved effective in transforming doubt into positive action. Learning from past triumphs enhances the ability to replicate success in the face of doubt.

4. Embracing Uncertainty as a Catalyst:

Doubt often arises in uncertain situations. Embracing uncertainty as a catalyst for growth involves reframing doubt as a natural response to the unknown. Rather than fearing uncertainty, individuals can view it as an opportunity for exploration, learning, and adaptation. This shift in perspective transforms doubt from a hindrance into a motivational force for navigating the unpredictable.

5. Cultivating a Growth Mindset:

A growth mindset sees challenges, including doubt, as opportunities for learning and development. Cultivating a growth mindset involves embracing the belief that abilities can be developed through effort and perseverance. By viewing doubt as a stepping stone to improvement, individuals foster resilience and motivation in the face of uncertainty.

6. Seeking Support and Feedback:

Doubt can be alleviated through external support and constructive feedback. Seeking guidance from mentors, friends, or colleagues provides valuable perspectives and insights. Constructive feedback not only helps individuals gain clarity on their doubts but also instills a sense of encouragement and motivation to push through challenges.

REAL-LIFE STORIES OF DOUBT TRANSFORMATION:

1. Rachel's Journey from Doubt to Empowerment:

Rachel faced self-doubt in pursuing a career change. By reframing doubt as a natural part of growth, setting incremental goals, and seeking support from a mentor, Rachel transformed her uncertainty into motivation. Her story illustrates the transformative power of leveraging doubt for personal and professional empowerment.

2. Mark's Triumph over Doubt in Entrepreneurship:

Mark experienced doubt when launching his entrepreneurial venture. Instead of succumbing to uncertainty, Mark embraced doubt as a driving force for innovation. Through learning from past doubt-driven successes, cultivating a growth mindset, and seeking feedback, Mark turned doubt into motivation, ultimately achieving success in his entrepreneurial endeavors.

OVERCOMING DOUBT IN SPECIFIC CONTEXTS:

1. Doubt in Creative Pursuits:

Doubt is common in creative endeavors, where self-expression and originality are paramount. This section explores strategies for transforming doubt into motivation in artistic, writing, or other creative pursuits. Embracing doubt as a natural part of the creative process and leveraging it to fuel inspiration are central themes.

2. Doubt in Professional Advancement:

Doubt often surfaces when individuals aim for career advancement or take on new responsibilities. Strategies for overcoming doubt in professional contexts include setting career goals, seeking mentorship, and recognizing doubt as a normal aspect of growth. Transforming doubt into motivation becomes a powerful tool for achieving professional success.

"Doubt can only be removed by action."

- Johann Wolfgang von Goethe

Chapter 12

MINDFULNESS PRACTICES FOR DAILY LIFE

In the hustle and bustle of modern living, incorporating mindfulness practices into daily life becomes a transformative journey toward enhanced well-being and a more profound connection with the present moment. This chapter explores the essence of mindfulness, delves into various mindfulness practices, and provides practical insights on integrating mindfulness into the fabric of everyday existence.

UNDERSTANDING THE ESSENCE OF MINDFULNESS:

Mindfulness, rooted in ancient contemplative traditions, has emerged as a powerful tool for navigating the complexities of contemporary life. At its core, mindfulness involves cultivating a heightened awareness of the present moment, embracing experiences without judgment, and fostering a non-reactive and accepting mindset.

The Science Behind Mindfulness:

Scientific research has underscored the profound impact of mindfulness on mental and physical health. Studies reveal that regular mindfulness practice can reduce stress, improve focus and attention, enhance emotional regulation, and contribute to overall well-being. The neuroscientific basis of mindfulness highlights its influence on brain structures associated with self-awareness, empathy, and emotional processing.

Embarking on Mindfulness Practices:

1. Mindful Breathing:

Mindful breathing serves as a foundational practice, anchoring attention to the rhythm of the breath. By directing focus to the inhalation and exhalation, individuals cultivate a sense of presence. The simplicity of this practice makes it accessible for beginners and a potent tool for fostering a calm and centered mind.

2. Body Scan Meditation:

Body scan meditation involves systematically directing attention to different parts of the body, cultivating awareness of sensations, and promoting a mind-body connection. This practice enhances bodily awareness, relaxes tense muscles, and encourages a deepening sense of mindfulness.

3. Observing Thoughts and Emotions:

Mindfulness invites individuals to observe thoughts and emotions without attachment or judgment. Through this practice, individuals develop a heightened awareness of their mental and emotional landscape, fostering a non-reactive stance toward the ebb and flow of thoughts and feelings.

4. Walking Meditation:

Walking meditation integrates mindfulness into motion, transforming a routine activity into a contemplative practice. By paying attention to each step, the sensation of movement, and the surrounding environment, individuals cultivate mindfulness in motion, promoting a sense of grounded presence.

5. Mindful Eating:

Mindful eating encourages a conscious and present approach to the act of eating. By savoring each bite, attending to flavors and textures, and appreciating the nourishment received, individuals foster a healthier relationship with food and deepen their connection with the sensory experience of eating.

6. Loving-Kindness Meditation:

Loving-kindness meditation, or Metta, involves cultivating feelings of love and compassion towards oneself and others. Through intentional phrases and heartfelt intentions, individuals expand their capacity for empathy, kindness, and connection, fostering a positive and inclusive mindset.

7. Mindful Communication:

Mindful communication emphasizes active listening, present-moment awareness, and empathetic response. By bringing mindfulness into conversations, individuals enhance the quality of their interactions, deepen understanding, and cultivate more meaningful connections with others.

INTEGRATING MINDFULNESS INTO DAILY ACTIVITIES:

1. Mindful Morning Routine:

Infusing mindfulness into the morning routine sets a positive tone for the day. Practices such as mindful breathing, gentle stretching, or a brief meditation can be incorporated into activities like showering, dressing, or having breakfast, promoting a centered and intentional start to the day.

2. Mindful Work Practices:

Mindfulness can be seamlessly woven into the fabric of work activities. Short mindfulness breaks, mindful breathing exercises, or incorporating moments of awareness during routine tasks can enhance focus, reduce stress, and contribute to a more balanced and productive work environment.

3. Mindful Commuting:

Commuting, often seen as a mundane and stressful activity, can become an opportunity for mindfulness. Whether driving, walking, or using public transportation, individuals can bring attention to the sensory experience of the journey, fostering a sense of calm amidst the hustle of daily life.

4. Mindfulness During Daily Tasks:

Mundane daily tasks, such as washing dishes, doing laundry, or cleaning, offer ample opportunities for mindfulness. By engaging fully in the present moment, and attending to sensations and movements, individuals can turn routine chores into mindful practices, cultivating a sense of presence in everyday activities.

5. Mindfulness in Leisure Activities:

Leisure activities, whether reading, gardening, or engaging in hobbies, can be enriched by mindfulness. By immersing fully in the experience, appreciating sensory details, and letting go of distractions, individuals can derive more enjoyment and fulfillment from their leisure pursuits.

Overcoming Challenges in Mindfulness Practice:

1. Dealing with Restlessness and Distraction:

Restlessness and distraction are common challenges in mindfulness practice. Techniques such as gently redirecting attention, using anchors like the breath, and acknowledging distractions without judgment help individuals navigate these challenges and deepen their mindfulness practice.

2. Cultivating Patience in the Process:

Patience is a key virtue in mindfulness practice. Acknowledging that the journey toward mindfulness is gradual and requires consistent effort allows individuals to approach the process with patience and self-compassion. Each moment of awareness contributes to the cumulative impact of mindfulness over time.

3. Balancing Mindfulness with Technology:

In an era dominated by technology, balancing mindfulness with screen time poses a unique challenge. Establishing mindful technology use practices, incorporating digital detox periods, and creating tech-free zones contribute to a more intentional and balanced relationship with technology.

4. Adapting Mindfulness to Individual Preferences:

Mindfulness is a flexible practice that can be adapted to individual preferences and lifestyles. Whether through guided meditations, silent contemplation, or movement-based practices like yoga, individuals can explore and choose mindfulness modalities that resonate with their unique preferences and needs.

REALIZING THE BENEFITS OF MINDFULNESS:

1. Stress Reduction and Relaxation:

Mindfulness practices are renowned for their stress-reducing effects. By fostering a calm and centered state of mind, individuals experience relaxation, reduced physiological stress responses, and an enhanced ability to cope with life's challenges.

2. Improved Focus and Concentration:

Regular mindfulness practice has been linked to improvements in cognitive functions, including focus and concentration. The cultivation of sustained attention and present-moment awareness contributes to heightened cognitive abilities and a more focused mind.

3. Enhanced Emotional Well-Being:

Mindfulness plays a pivotal role in emotional regulation. By cultivating a non-reactive and accepting stance towards emotions, individuals experience increased emotional resilience, greater emotional intelligence, and a more balanced emotional well-being.

4. Greater Self-Awareness:

Mindfulness fosters self-awareness by encouraging individuals to observe their thoughts, emotions, and behaviors without judgment. This heightened self-awareness facilitates personal growth, enhanced self-understanding, and the ability to make conscious choices aligned with one's values.

5. Cultivation of Compassion and Empathy:

Mindfulness practices, particularly loving-kindness meditation, contribute to the cultivation of compassion and empathy. By expanding one's capacity for understanding and kindness, individuals foster more positive and harmonious relationships with themselves and others.

6. Improved Sleep Quality:

Mindfulness has shown positive effects on sleep quality. Practices such as mindful breathing or body scan meditation can promote relaxation, reduce bedtime anxiety, and contribute to improved sleep patterns, enhancing overall sleep quality.

7. Mindfulness and Physical Health:

The mind-body connection is evident in the positive impact of mindfulness on physical health. Research indicates that mindfulness practices can lower blood pressure, improve immune function, and contribute to overall physical well-being.

OVERCOMING COMMON MISCONCEPTIONS ABOUT MINDFULNESS:

1. Mindfulness is Not Just Sitting in Silence:

Contrary to the misconception that mindfulness is solely about sitting in silence, it encompasses a variety of practices, including movement-based activities, mindful eating, and even engaging in daily tasks with full awareness. Mindfulness is a versatile and adaptable approach to cultivating present-moment awareness.

2. Mindfulness is More than Relaxation:

While relaxation is a common outcome of mindfulness, its scope extends beyond stress reduction. Mindfulness involves cultivating a profound awareness of the present moment, fostering a non-judgmental attitude, and enhancing overall well-being. Relaxation is a byproduct rather than the sole objective of mindfulness.

3. Mindfulness is Not about Suppressing Thoughts:

Mindfulness does not aim to suppress thoughts or achieve a state of thoughtlessness. Instead, it encourages individuals to observe thoughts without attachment or judgment. The goal is to develop a non-reactive stance towards thoughts, allowing them to come and go without undue influence.

4. Mindfulness is Attainable for Everyone:

Mindfulness is a practice that is accessible to individuals of all ages, backgrounds, and lifestyles. Whether practiced for a few minutes or longer durations, mindfulness can be tailored to suit individual preferences. The key is consistency and a willingness to engage in the process.

<u>**MINDFULNESS IN THE CONTEXT OF SPECIFIC LIFE CHALLENGES:**</u>

1. Mindfulness in Coping with Anxiety:

Anxiety often involves concerns about the future or rumination on past events. Mindfulness provides tools for anchoring attention to the present moment, reducing excessive worry, and cultivating a more peaceful relationship with the uncertainties of life.

2. Mindfulness in Stressful Work Environments:

In the demanding landscape of modern workplaces, mindfulness offers a refuge. Practices such as brief mindfulness breaks, mindful breathing, and cultivating a mindful approach to tasks contribute to stress reduction and increased resilience in the face of workplace challenges.

3. Mindfulness in Enhancing Creativity:

Creativity flourishes in a mindful state. By quieting the mind, reducing mental chatter, and fostering an open and receptive mindset, individuals can enhance their creative capacities. Mindfulness practices become a conduit for unlocking innovative thinking and creative expression.

4. Mindfulness in Relationship Dynamics:

Mindfulness practices can transform interpersonal relationships. By bringing mindful communication, empathetic listening, and non-reactive awareness into relationships, individuals foster deeper connections, navigate conflicts more skillfully, and contribute to the overall well-being of their relational dynamics.

"The present moment is filled with joy and happiness. If you are attentive, you will see it."

- Thich Nhat Hanh

Chapter 13:

THE ART OF SAYING 'NO'

Mastering the delicate skill of saying 'no' is an art that holds profound implications for personal well-being, productivity, and the cultivation of healthy relationships. This chapter explores the nuances of assertiveness, the psychology behind people-pleasing tendencies, and practical strategies for setting boundaries. From understanding the impact of 'no' on mental health to navigating social and professional scenarios, embracing the art of saying 'no' empowers individuals to reclaim their time, prioritize self-care, and foster authentic connections.

UNDERSTANDING THE PSYCHOLOGY OF PEOPLE-PLEASING:

1. The Urge to Please:

The desire to please others is deeply rooted in human psychology, often stemming from a need for approval and fear of rejection. This section delves into the psychological underpinnings of people-pleasing tendencies, exploring how societal expectations, childhood experiences, and self-esteem influence the compulsion to say 'yes' even when it may not align with one's needs.

2. The Fear of Disapproval:

Fear of disapproval is a common driver behind the reluctance to say 'no.' This section examines how the fear of being perceived as uncooperative or disappointing others can lead individuals to prioritize external validation over their well-being. Understanding this fear is pivotal in dismantling the barriers to assertiveness.

3. Boundaries and Self-Worth:

The ability to say 'no' is intricately linked to the establishment of healthy boundaries. This section explores how setting and maintaining boundaries is a reflection of one's self-worth and a crucial aspect of cultivating healthy relationships. Insights into recognizing and addressing boundary violations contribute to the development of assertiveness.

THE POWER OF SAYING 'NO' FOR MENTAL HEALTH:

1. The Impact on Stress and Burnout:

Relentlessly saying 'yes' to every demand can lead to heightened stress levels and eventual burnout. This section delves into the psychological and physiological consequences of chronic people-pleasing, emphasizing the liberating impact of 'no' in mitigating stress and preserving mental well-being.

2. Prioritizing Self-Care:

Saying 'no' is an act of prioritizing self-care, a cornerstone of mental and emotional resilience. This section explores how establishing boundaries and practicing self-care contribute to overall well-being. Practical strategies for incorporating self-care into daily life and the role of saying 'no' in this process are discussed.

3. Authenticity and Personal Integrity:

The ability to say 'no' authentically is a manifestation of personal integrity. This section examines the alignment between one's values, beliefs, and actions, emphasizing how embracing authenticity fosters a sense of empowerment and contributes to a more fulfilling life.

NAVIGATING SOCIAL AND PROFESSIONAL SCENARIOS:

1. Saying 'No' in Personal Relationships:

The dynamics of personal relationships often pose unique challenges when it comes to saying 'no.' This section explores strategies for navigating assertiveness in friendships, family dynamics, and romantic relationships. Insights into communicating boundaries effectively without compromising the quality of relationships are discussed.

2. Assertiveness in the Workplace:

The professional sphere presents its own set of challenges in asserting boundaries. This section delves into the art of saying 'no' in the workplace, addressing scenarios such as managing workload, declining additional responsibilities, and setting limits on time commitments. Strategies for maintaining professional relationships while prioritizing personal boundaries are explored.

3. Dealing with Guilt and Rejection:

Guilt often accompanies the act of saying 'no,' especially when it involves rejecting requests or declining invitations. This section examines the psychology of guilt and strategies for reframing guilt-inducing thoughts. Insights into navigating the fear of rejection and recognizing that setting boundaries is a valid act of self-preservation are discussed.

1. The Gentle Art of Declining:

Saying 'no' need not be confrontational or harsh. This section explores the nuances of the gentle art of declining, emphasizing the power of diplomatic language, expressing gratitude, and offering alternatives. Practical examples and scripts for gracefully declining requests are provided.

2. Setting Clear and Assertive Boundaries:

Assertiveness is key to effective boundary-setting. This section delves into the principles of assertive communication, including clear and direct expression of one's needs, wants, and limits. Strategies for maintaining composure and confidence while setting boundaries are discussed.

3. Learning to Prioritize:

Prioritization is at the heart of effective time and energy management. This section explores the art of discerning between urgent and important tasks, aligning commitments with personal and professional goals, and making intentional choices. Insights into the value of saying 'no' as a strategic decision-making tool are discussed.

4. Building a Supportive Network:

Having a supportive network is instrumental in navigating the challenges of saying 'no.' This section explores the importance of surrounding oneself with understanding and respectful individuals. Insights into communicating boundaries with empathy and building relationships that honor mutual respect are discussed.

Real-Life Stories of Saying 'No' Success:

1. Emma's Journey to Assertiveness:

Emma struggled with chronic people-pleasing, often feeling overwhelmed by excessive commitments. Through self-reflection and the gradual practice of saying 'no,' Emma transformed her life. Her story illustrates the transformative power of embracing assertiveness and setting boundaries for personal well-being.

2. James' Professional Boundary Mastery:

James faced challenges in the workplace, juggling numerous responsibilities without the ability to decline additional tasks. Through assertive communication and strategic boundary-setting, James not only alleviated his workload but also gained the respect of colleagues and superiors. His success highlights the impact of saying 'no' in a professional context.

<u>THE ART OF SAYING 'NO' IN SPECIFIC SCENARIOS:</u>

1. Saying 'No' to Social Obligations:

Social obligations often present opportunities for practicing assertiveness. This section explores strategies for gracefully declining social invitations, managing FOMO (Fear of Missing Out), and fostering authentic connections by aligning social commitments with personal values.

2. Declining Unreasonable Work Requests:

In a professional setting, saying 'no' to unreasonable work requests is essential for maintaining a healthy work-life balance. This section

provides practical tips for communicating limitations, negotiating workload, and navigating professional expectations without compromising personal well-being.

"Saying 'no' can be the ultimate self-care." - Claudia Black

CONCLUSION

"How to Train Your Brain to Overcome Fear and Doubt: Stop Overthinking, Build Our Mindset" serves as a comprehensive guide to empower individuals on their journey towards personal development and emotional resilience. From understanding the intricate nature of fear and doubt to unraveling the psychology behind overthinking, each chapter offers valuable insights and practical strategies for fostering a positive mindset. The exploration of neuroplasticity, the brain's role, and the art of saying 'no' provides a holistic approach to mental well-being. The inclusion of real-life stories, quotes, and diverse scenarios enhances the relatability and applicability of the content. As readers navigate the realms of self-discovery and growth, the book emphasizes the importance of embracing challenges, cultivating mindfulness, and building assertiveness. Ultimately, the overarching message is one of empowerment, encouraging individuals to take charge of their thoughts, emotions, and actions, and to cultivate a balanced and empowered mindset that transcends fear and doubt. As we conclude this transformative journey, the chapters collectively serve as a roadmap for readers to sustain a positive mindset in the long run, fostering resilience and contributing to a more fulfilling life.